Beats & Company

Also by Ann Charters

Nobody: The Story of Bert Williams
Olson/Melville: A Study in Affinity
Kerouac: A Biography

Editor

Scenes Along the Road: Photographs of the
 Desolation Angels, 1944-1960
The Special View of History: Charles Olson's
 Lectures at Black Mountain College
Scattered Poems by Jack Kerouac
The Beats: Literary Bohemians in Postwar America

Beats & Company

A Portrait of a Literary Generation

by
Ann Charters

A DOLPHIN BOOK
Doubleday & Company, Inc.
Garden City, New York
1986

The black and white images were printed, and the
book conceived and designed, by Samuel Charters.

Thanks to the University of Connecticut Research Foundation
for partial funding for travel to California and Oregon to work
on this project.

Acknowledgments

Ted Berrigan, *Many Happy Returns.* Copyright © 1969 by Ted Berrigan. Reprinted by
permission of Corinth Books.

Gregory Corso, *The Happy Birthday of Death.* Copyright © 1960 by Gregory Corso.
Reprinted by permission of New Directions Publishing Corporation.

Diane di Prima, *Loba.* Copyright © 1978 by Diane di Prima. Reprinted by permission of
Wingbow Press.

Allen Ginsberg, *Kaddish.* Copyright © 1961 by Allen Ginsberg. Reprinted by permission of
the author and Harper & Row.

Louis Ginsberg, *Morning in Spring.* Copyright © 1970 by Louis Ginsberg. Reprinted by
permission of William Morrow & Company, Inc.

Jack Kerouac, *Doctor Sax.* Copyright © 1959 by Jack Kerouac. Reprinted by permission of
Grove Press, Inc.

Charles Olson, *The Maximus Poems.* Copyright © 1960 by Charles Olson. Reprinted by
permission of the Regents of the University of California.

Peter Orlovsky, *Clean Asshole Poems & Smiling Vegetable Songs.* Copyright © 1978 by Peter
Orlovsky. Reprinted by permission of City Lights Books.

Gary Snyder, *The Back Country.* Copyright © 1968 by Gary Snyder. Reprinted by permission of New Directions Publishing Corporation.

Library of Congress Cataloging-in-Publication Data

Charters, Ann.
    Beats & Company.   810.9
                                        C486

    "A Dolphin book."
    Includes index.
    1. American literature—20th century—History and
criticism—Pictorial works.   2. Bohemianism—United
States—Pictorial works.   3. Authors, American—20th
century—Portraits.   I. Title.   II. Title: Beats and
company.
PS228.B6C48   1986   810'.9'0054   86-4479
ISBN 0-385-23368-X

To-

The memory of Lee D. Witkin
and Kate Schultz Danberg

Introduction

by
John Clellon Holmes

Most good photographs result from accident or artifice. The camera was at the ready when the decisive moment came or the photographer saw a perfect composition and waited for the perfect light. But a great photograph, one that illuminates its viewer as well as its subject, happens when the senses and the insights of the photographer intersect at the instant of the *click*, and a personal statement broaches the neutrality of the lens. It's what Thoreau was getting at when he wrote: "The highest we can attain to is not Knowledge, but Sympathy with Intelligence."

Ann Charters has it. Best known as a literary biographer and critic (of Jack Kerouac, Vladimir Mayakovsky, and Charles Olson), now, with this stunning book of portraits of the Beat writers, she is revealed, more or less in a flash (though she doesn't use one), as a photographer whose work exemplifies Thoreau's equation. In picture after picture, she seems to have come to her subject neither to praise or blame, but to *perceive* her way towards vision via the camera.

Using a Rollieflex, and occasionally a Nikon, working with what she likes to call "non-available light," chiaroscuro dominates her eye. Light and shadow suggest the shifting equivocations of her subject's relationship to mortality rather than the hard-edge Either/Or of photojournalism. Alfred Steiglitz and Julia Margaret Cameron are her mentors—the Steiglitz who looked for the vein of poetry in the drab slag of life, the Cameron who insisted on finding her own image her own way.

Sam Charters, Ann's husband, himself a poet and novelist, has worked alchemical miracles in the darkroom. He created the prints and designed the book. The emotional clarity of the pictures is a tribute to a collaboration between two people who are married in their intentions as well as before the law. Together, they have made images of the stream-bed that sometimes shines up, lucid and fleeting, through the roiled waters of the writing life.

Ann Charters
Photo by Raymond Ross

The Beat writers may be the most photographed literary group in American history. For decades now, they have been snapped at parties and readings, on the street or in the loft, off guard or on their muscle. Cameras snooped on them because they were felt to be news of an extra literary sort, and they became the first group of writers to be treated to the dubious media attention usually reserved for rock stars. But you rarely got the impression that the photographers knew Beat writing well, or understood why the writers themselves might be truly newsworthy. Counter lifestyles were what was wanted, not glimpses into the creative spirit, and what was caught were surfaces.

Clearly, Ann Charters has not only read the work, but is keen to its challenges and meanings. She is patient, unintimidated by deadlines and unsatisfied with snap judgements. She has a point of view, not just a good angle. She believes these people are more consequential as writers than as "celebrities." Her portraits depict serious artists, caught mostly alone as artists mostly are, with their public guards, but not their psychic pants, down. Hers is a sensitive, questioning eye that suggests a decency of character that is rarer than talent, the eye of a thoughtful observer rather than a scandal-avid *paparazzi*. What she has waited for, and what these writers have ultimately given her, and what she is savvy enough to recognize, are those privileged moments when the inner life glimmers up through the face.

If you've been photographed overmuch, being "shot" by Ann Charters can be a disarming experience. She does not arrive bandoliered with cameras. She is not briskly dictatorial nor aimlessly chatty. She doesn't order you about, or reorganize your house in the interests of the light meter. She sits, and maybe has a glass of wine, and talks. Her talk is good, and your talk gets good as a result. She knows who you are, she has read your work, she is a stimulating and attractive companion, and by the end of the meeting when the camera comes out, you are relaxed, opened by the pith and sense of her questions, and the conversation goes on while she does her work, and then—it is over. You realize that you have had a pleasant experience of which the picture-taking was only a part. You do not feel, as so many people from cameraless cultures do, that she has "stolen your soul". Later, you discover that you are wrong.

I've known most of the people in this book for years. I've been badgered by the same batteries of cameras, I've sniffed at the mostly graceless results, and I've made my peace with the obdurate fact that what I valued in my friends and colleagues wasn't going to be captured on film. But here it is.

Here is the late Kerouac—pugnacious, stubborn, confused, sad at heart, his once-vernal spirit in deep autumn. The picture of him kneeling behind his mother, features coarsened by age and abuse yet starkly expressive of the fatalism and resignation of a man in the twilight of his life, is moving beyond words, as classic and revealing as the famous *Madmoiselle* photo of ten years earlier, and truer to the pensive Jack who wrote the books.

Here is Allen Ginsberg in his many guises—the baffled farmer of Cherry Valley wondering why the crops don't grow, the diligent tyro-Schweitzer hunched over the organ feeling for a final chord, the respectful son, posing, poet to poet, with his hand on his father's shoulder—Ginsberg the tireless affirmer of the old continuities.

Here is the massive physicality of Charles Olson, a Gulliver in the alleys of Gloucester, poetry's only rogue elephant after Pound, heavy and passionate of mind. Here is the best picture of Gary Snyder that I have seen, puckish, canny, the smile lines indented in his face by work and weather and some private gaiety of soul. Here is Bill Burroughs looking like a haunted, anonymous minor official, who has just planted a bogus time bomb in the paranoid streets of Kafka. Here, too, is the most piquant photograph of Gregory Corso, for once not cavorting or mugging, but climbing the laborious steps (of need? of aspiration?) with besieged yet trusting eyes. Here is Peter Orlovsky like a stern-faced *raskolnik* out of Dostoyevski, and Larry Ferlinghetti the poetic Little Father of *City Lights,* and marvelous Ken Kesey exuding energy like sweat—and so many others.

And here, finally, are the pictures at Kerouac's graveside that ache with the differing faces of grief, the mourners unaware of how vulnerable they have suddenly become, the last poignancy of October adding a shiver to the mood, and—but what more need be said? Here, too, the composite shot on the porch of the Columbine Lodge in Boulder, Colorado (thirteen years later), during the Naropa Celebration of the 25th Anniversary of the publication of *On the Road,* everyone for one poised moment staring into those long thoughts that reunions evoke, moody with the momentary stillness that invades divergent lives brought together after too long a time.

In each picture, Ann Charters has waited for the masks to drop so the private face could come clear, and she has not intruded on it so much as been a tactful witness to its presence.

Now some of us have died, a few of us have strayed, and all of us are aging. But it was art, and art's chance at truth, that we were after all along, and Ann Charters' sympathetic intelligence has caught and respected that. Put simply, these are the best portraits of the Beat writers that will probably ever be made.

A Note on the Photographs

by
Ann Charters

I took my first photograph of a Beat writer on a Sunday afternoon in early June 1966 when I walked over to Allen Ginsberg's apartment in a tenement building on Tenth Street in New York City's Lower East Side. It wasn't the first time I'd met a Beat writer, and it wasn't the first time I'd taken my camera when I was going to talk to someone, but the collection of photographs that became this book originated that Sunday afternoon with Allen Ginsberg.

By 1966 Ginsberg had been the focus of a lot of cameras, and he wasn't much interested in having me take his picture. To get his attention I began to ask him questions about Kerouac's writing. I launched into a long question about the books making up what Kerouac called his "Legend of Duluoz." When I stopped, Ginsberg started to talk, and what he said was so thought-provoking, I put my camera bag on the floor, rummaged for my pencil and notebook, and an interview was in progress.

A half hour later the phone rang. I was disappointed when Allen broke off to answer it. Sitting cross-legged on a mattress, he looked up at me. "It's Dylan," he explained. Whereupon he gave Bob Dylan the same undivided attention he had previously given me. I sensed the phone call would go on awhile, so I began to walk around the apartment.

Peter Orlovsky was reading a book in the room next door. I asked him if I could take his picture, and got out my camera. He was shyer than Allen, not looking straight at me, preferring to gaze out the window or down at his book. After a few pictures I went back to Allen, still deep in conversation with Dylan, smoking a cigarette while he talked. He didn't seem bothered by my taking pictures. I finished the roll of film in the Rolleiflex just after he put down the telephone. I didn't know it, but I was embarked on a photographic project that would occupy me for the next twenty years.

It wasn't, as I said, the first time I'd met Beat writers. Though Peter didn't remember, I'd met him ten years before in Berkeley in the spring of 1956, when I was a nineteen-year-old undergraduate at the University of California. My roommate, an art student from Mill Valley named Carolyn Cain, had friends in San Francisco, and she fixed me up through someone she knew with Peter Orlovsky as a blind date.

Peter showed up one evening on the porch of the co-op off Dwight Way where I was living, a tall, blond twenty-two year old whom Kerouac later called "Simon Darlovsky" in *Desolation Angels*. We walked a couple of miles to a spaghetti party at a Berkeley cottage on Milvia Street below Telegraph Avenue, getting there too late to get much spaghetti but in good time to crowd into a car with a group of people from the party to drive to a poetry reading where, Peter explained, his good friend the poet Allen Ginsberg was going to perform.

At the theater where the reading was to take place, Peter's friends went off to get the stage ready while he showed me the large black and white drawings hanging on the walls, an exhibition by the San Francisco artist Robert LaVigne featuring Peter and Allen Ginsberg making love. I remember the drawings baffled me—I didn't understand anything about them. Why would two men let an artist draw them making love and then let the drawings be shown in public? I didn't ask Peter to explain. He was obviously very proud of the drawings. I didn't know that he and Allen were still lovers and would continue to live together for years.

I wish I had taken a camera with me that night to the poetry reading, not only to photograph the event but also to document the appearance of LaVigne's drawings, which were stolen shortly afterward by someone less naive than I was. But I didn't own a camera in April 1956, and I didn't know that the evening would be remembered years later as an historic event, the repetition of an even more famous reading the previous October in San Francisco advertised as "Six Poets at the Six Gallery," where Ginsberg introduced his poem *Howl*.

The five other poets—Kenneth Rexroth, Gary Snyder, Michael McClure, Philip Lamantia and Philip Whalen—were on stage in the Berkeley theater to repeat their performances along with Ginsberg that evening. The program was again a great success, the audience filling the little theater clapping and cheering the poets as they read their work in what seemed to me to be the spirit of marvelous poetry vaudeville. Neal Cassady was in the audience that night, but I was most taken with Jack Kerouac—Peter pointed him out to me. He was impossible to miss, a dark-haired, extremely handsome man who stood out in the crowd in front of the stage urging people to contribute money for the jugs of California wine which he helped keep circulating up and down the aisles.

I bought my first camera eighteen months later, after I graduated college and took my first full-time job. I don't remember why I bought the camera—a secondhand fold-out Kodak in a worn leather case which I'd seen in a shop window in Berkeley. I certainly didn't have photographs of the Beat writers in mind at the time, though *Howl* and *On the Road* were recently published and City Lights Bookshop in San Francisco was a place that my friend Sam Charters sometimes took me to browse. I didn't even take any pictures of Sam with my camera before he left Berkeley late in 1957 and rode the Greyhound to New Orleans to record the Eureka Brass Band.

Not long after that the circumstances of my life changed. With a Woodrow Wilson Fellowship I left California to attend graduate school at Columbia University, and with Sam's encouragement I began taking photographs seriously. In the summer of 1958 I traveled with him to the out islands of the Bahamas to document the music still surviving in the isolated settlements there. One morning at Fresh Creek Harbor I saw the hand-built boats pulled up on the beach during low tide. I was alone with my Kodak in hand, and for no reason I clearly understood, I felt the urge to take a picture. I waded into the water until the image in the viewfinder felt right, and then I took a picture of the stern of one of the boats lying on its side. It became the cover for the first phonograph album Folkways Records released of our Bahamian recordings six months later, right after Sam and I were married. It was my first published photograph.

For the next nine years I went on using the camera to help Sam in his fieldwork documenting black music. He produced records and articles and books, all of them needing photographs. I was so busy with my own graduate studies and Sam's photos that I didn't seek out other assignments or think of exhibitions. Our friend the musicologist and photographer Fred Ramsey had told us to use a professional lab to develop the negatives, but most of them were put away unprinted for years.

By 1965 the camera had become so much a part of what I did that when I completed my doctoral dissertation at Columbia University on the American writers who had lived in the Berkshires, I included a photographic essay on the Berkshire landscape as evidence of the region's literary history. The essay was never published, though some of the photos became album covers for Folkways recordings of Charles Ives' music, and a group of prints was included in a "construct" describing Herman Melville's life in Pittsfield, Massachusetts, that was issued by our small publishing company, Portents.

By then I had traded in my Kodak. The cameras I used were a Pentax 35 mm (later sold for a Nikon) and a Rolleiflex. The Rollei was my favorite, despite the difficulty of focusing it accurately on indoor subjects using only available light. My struggle with its depth of field when the lens was wide open reminded me of the earlier heroic endeavors of the pioneer English

photographer Julia Margaret Cameron, who had great success with out-of-focus pictures. She always focused her lens on something which to her eye was very beautiful, instead of going on to get a more definite focus on the entire picture.

I preferred the Rollei to the other cameras because it seemed to me that the Rollei lens registered the way I saw my subjects most truthfully. In one of her short stories Flannery O'Connor writes about the sun coming out to make everything in nature appear in its "true light." When O'Connor described it, she implied that the "true light" was harsh and uncompromising. For me this "true light" is something else. The light I worked in was often too dim and full of shadows to get a razor-sharp focus, but in some inexplicable manner the tones related in the finished portrait the way I saw my subjects revealed in my mind's eye the moment when I stood opposite them close enough to talk and pressed the shutter.

Ann Charters with Allen Ginsberg, 1967
Photo by Herbert Huncke

Perhaps you could say that the gathering of photographs in *Beats & Company* had its origin in a project begun a few weeks earlier than the Sunday I went over to East Tenth Street to talk to Allen Ginsberg. Sam and I had moved to an apartment in the East Village on St. Mark's Place, already engaged in the demonstrations that were beginning to protest the Vietnam War. In the spring of 1966, while Sam was traveling around the world, I borrowed a friend's Nagra tape recorder to record a poetry reading not far from our apartment at St. Mark's Church in the Bowery. It was an evening entitled "Poems for Peace," and nearly every Underground poet in New York showed up to read: Allen Ginsberg, Peter Orlovsky, Ed Sanders, Tuli Kupferberg, Jackson MacLow, and many others. Since I thought it was too dark in the church to photograph—I was too busy running the tape recorder to concentrate on taking pictures—I decided to contact the poets after the reading to get their portraits for an album cover when the tapes were released as a record. I edited the tapes and set out to take the photographs with my Rollei. Ginsberg was first.

The conversation and photographs with him and Peter in June 1966 initiated my work with the Beat writers and others in their literary circle. After that session I photographed the other New York poets on the "Poems for Peace" record, among them Ed Sanders, Paul Blackburn and Jackson MacLow. Then my next project, inspired partly by Allen's comments on Jack's writing, was a bibliography of the works of Jack Kerouac, compiled at the request of Robert A. Wilson, who was issuing the Phoenix Bookshop's series of bibliographies of contemporary writers. Bob Wilson advised me to write Kerouac's mother Gabrielle for permission to come to her home to catalog Jack's books, since she had the best collection of them.

Jack Kerouac invited me to visit him and his mother in Hyannis, Massachusetts, in August 1966. I took along my Rolleiflex, but at first Jack refused to be photographed. After working with him for two days compiling the bibliography, he gave his permission for a few pictures just before I packed up to leave. I loaded a roll of Tri-x in the camera and photographed him in his bedroom, eight quick shots. Then he asked me to photograph his mother. She came out of the kitchen in her apron, and I suggested that she make herself comfortable in a chair in the living room. One of Jack's favorite cats jumped in her lap as I took three pictures. Jack stood by, watching.

Before I took the last exposure on the roll of film , I asked him to get into the picture with his mother and the cat. Without a word he kneeled down in back of her chair, cradling his cheek in his left fist. There was almost no light on the meter reading, but I didn't want to fuss with the drapes behind them. This photograph is one of my favorites, the only one I have ever seen that suggests the deep, tangled bond of love and helpless dependency between Jack and his mother. He called her his "best girl," the woman who kept house for him and supported his writing all his life.

The same summer I also photographed another writer whose work I greatly admired, the poet Charles Olson. He was living alone in Gloucester, Massachusetts, after his wife's death in an automobile accident. Olson shook his head when I told him I had been working with Kerouac on his bibliography. "Why do you want to waste your time with that Canuck?" he growled, half serious.

It was a good question. I liked Kerouac's books and the work of others in the counterculture group of the literary Underground because I responded to what they were writing in an immediate, personal way. Trained as an academic, theoretically I should have been doing research on Establishment writers such as Samuel Beckett, W. H. Auden, Saul Bellow, or Robert Lowell. But the content and style of the Underground writers like Kerouac and Ginsberg, Olson and Diane di Prima, appealed to me when I browsed among the recently published books in the New York bookstores. I respected them as artists because I shared their Romantic optimism and their political commitment, their nagging feeling that long ago something in America, as the dancer Merce Cunningham once expressed it to me, had gotten off on the wrong foot.

I didn't try to explain any of this to Olson, of course. Instead I jokingly told him I couldn't help myself; I was addicted to reading the books he and Kerouac wrote. So one afternoon he took me and my camera for a walk around his neighborhood in Gloucester on the streets close to the Atlantic Ocean. George Butterick, his bibliographer, came with us to keep Charles talking while I concentrated on the photographs, trying to capture a sense of the poet in his setting. At one point in our walk along the seawall, George dropped behind us and took our picture while I talked to Charles. In the photograph he towers more than a foot above me, gesturing with his hands as he glides over the pavement in his tennis shoes, engrossed in a description of how Merce Cunningham taught him to dance back in the old days at Black Mountain College.

Two years later, in July 1968, I went out to Berkeley to meet Robert Hawley, who had published my book on Olson's writing about Herman Melville—*Olson/Melville: A Study in Affinity*. Hawley had liked my photographs of Olson in Gloucester so much he had included a section of them in the book. He asked me to photograph some of the poets in the Bay Area whom he was publishing with his small press Oyez: David Meltzer, Mary Fabilli, and William Everson, who was then living as Brother Antoninus in a priory in Marin County.

After completing the Olson study and the Kerouac bibliography, I had embarked on an ambitious project that I conceived as a documentation of the Beat literary scene of the 1960s. The situation was complicated by the fact that Sam and I had our first child in June 1967. Three months after she was born I was also working full-time as a teacher during the tumultuous years of open enrollment in a New York City Community College.

If I had little time to write about the Beats, I felt I could capture a sense of them on film. The summer of 1969 I returned to San Francisco for another photographic session. On the West Coast in June 1969 I photographed the writers who were there at that time: Kenneth Rexroth, Robert Duncan, Lawrence Ferlinghetti, Gregory Corso, Michael McClure, Gary Snyder, and Donald M. Allen.

A month later I was back on the East Coast, photographing Olson's friend the poet Robert Creeley in Annisquam, Massachusetts, not far from Gloucester. Then, unexpectedly, Kerouac died in October 1969. A few days later Sam and I went to his funeral in Lowell, Massachusetts. I had been to that city several times to take pictures of Kerouac's neighborhood, thinking that one day I might want to write a literary study of his Legend of Duluoz, illustrated with photographs the way I had given a view of Olson's Gloucester neigh-

Walking with Charles Olson, 1968
Photo by George Butterick

borhood in *Olson/Melville*. But I was unprepared for Kerouac's sudden death at the age of forty-seven on October 21, 1969.

In Lowell, Kerouac's body lay in an open coffin at the Archambault Funeral Home. Oddly enough, I had photographed the tiles in the sidewalk spelling out the name of the funeral home on a previous trip. The next day I took pictures outside the church as the pallbearers carried the coffin up the steps for the service. Then I photographed Ginsberg, Corso and John Clellon Holmes at the cemetery, dropping a last flower into the grave before I turned away.

Olson died a few months later, in the bitter winter of 1970. I never brought my camera when Sam and I visited him in the Manhattan hospital where he was treated for cancer of the liver, though other people were taking pictures. Charles told me he admired my photographs of him in *Olson/Melville*, especially the one used as a frontispiece: "You're the only one who's captured my physicality." I asked him to tell me about the dreams he was having with the morphine in the hospital—he'd always wanted to hear about my dreams when we talked in Gloucester. But he said the saddest thing. "They've given me so much morphine, all my wires are crossed. I don't have dreams anymore." I didn't have the heart to go to Gloucester for his funeral. My father also died about this time, after a long illness. I developed an aversion to funerals.

After Kerouac and Olson died, I wanted my photographs to have a new dimension, documenting a broader sense of the writers' time and place, which I realize now was my instinctive attempt to connect them to what I felt was a more enduring landscape. I rode a Greyhound bus down to North Carolina to visit Black Mountain College where Olson had taught twenty years before, along with Robert Creeley, Merce Cunningham, the photographers Harry Callahan and Aaron Siskind, and many other experimental artists whose work I admired. One of the photos I took of the deserted college buildings became the cover for an Oyez book, *The Special View of History*, the last work I did with Olson before his death.

During the summer of 1970 I drove to upstate New York to visit Ginsberg on his farm in Cherry Valley. He had bought it as a place for him and Peter to live outside New York City, to get Peter out of what Allen called the "amphetamine hell" of the Lower East Side. Along with Peter and his brother Julius, I met the writers Ray and Bonnie Bremser and their daughter Georgia. Barry Miles and Gordon Ball, both helping Allen edit his papers, were also living at the farm that August, along with Ann Buchanan, Maretta Greer, and Peter's girlfriend Denise Felieu.

In blue jeans and a workshirt Allen walked me around outside the farm, showing me the pond and barn and haystacks, posing with little Georgia Bremser on his lap in the middle of a field of goldenrod. He seemed happiest inside the house practicing his music at the parlor organ, working on an album of Blake songs, setting *Songs of Innocence and of Experience* to his own melodies. The rules of keyboard harmony were uppermost on his mind at the time. I told him about Walter Piston's book on harmony, which I'd studied at Berkeley, but Ginsberg was more interested in figuring music out his own way.

My work with the Beats continued into the 1970s, though the new decade ushered in an important change in my life. In January 1971, after the Kent State tragedy and the Cambodian invasion, Sam and I and our three-year-old daughter moved to Stockholm, Sweden, as a personal protest against the Vietnam War. It seemed a natural culmination of all the peace demonstrations we had participated in during the preceding years. Sam began producing phonograph records for a Swedish company, but I was unable to find a teaching job. I stayed home and began writing a biography of Jack Kerouac with the notes I had compiled for my study of the Underground writers.

In 1974, after *Kerouac* was published, I returned to the United States to teach at the University of Connecticut. Sam and I had a second daughter, and both girls came with me to Connecticut. For several years we went back and forth between Sweden and America, while Sam and I worked together on a book about the Russian Futurist poet Vladimir Mayakovsky.

During the fall of 1980, while I was a Fulbright lecturer at Uppsala University in Sweden, Sam stayed in Connecticut to look after the children. In the long evenings in the country he fixed up a photographic darkroom in the basement of our house and began to print the negatives that had accumulated over the years. Since he was teaching himself how to work in a darkroom as he went along, I had no idea what he was finding until in one of his letters he enclosed a small print of a photograph of Kerouac I had taken fourteen years before but never seen printed. It was at that point that I realized what was there. The next year the library of the University of Connecticut at Storrs exhibited a group of the writers' portraits that Sam had printed. The following year the show was expanded at the Gotham Book Mart Gallery in New York City and then in the Butler Library at Columbia University.

In 1982 Sam and I were invited to participate in a conference at the Naropa Institute in Boulder, Colorado, celebrating the twenty-fifth anniversary of the publication of Kerouac's *On the Road*. We stayed at the Columbine Lodge at the Chatauqua compound on the edge of Boulder, a few miles from the center of town. The porch of the lodge became our meeting place, the center of our own private reunion with the writers who had been invited to the conference: John Clellon Holmes, Lawrence Ferlinghetti, Michael and Joanna McClure, Gregory Corso, Diane di Prima, Ted Berrigan, Carl Solomon, Carolyn Cassady, Joyce Johnson, Jack Micheline, and many others. Regardless of the hour, someone was always sitting on the porch waiting to talk, and in a chair I would often observe the photographer Robert Frank, who had done the movie *Pull My Daisy* with Kerouac, Ginsberg, Orlovsky, Corso, and their painter friend Larry Rivers years before. At the conference Robert Frank filmed the porch and its inhabitants, and I filmed him.

Why as a photographer have I thought the Beats were important enough to spend so much time on? At the beginning there was certainly the excitement of the writers just being there, the presence of a literary group around me writing books I wanted to read, filled with a passion for ideas and a belief in the value of spontaneity that I also shared. But newness wears off, and there had to be something else in their writing to hold my attention.

When I thought about it, I realized that there are definitions of the terms "modern" and "postmodern" which recognize that what we consider "modern" is more than just another term for "contemporary." The creation of "modern" art and literature was an attempt to save the world. It was moral and committed, the artist's spiritual quest expressed in secular terms. By breaking through the constrictions of the old ideas that had led to social injustices and world wars, the creators of "modern" art believed their work would express new ideas that would save us. "Postmodern" art doesn't have any of these connotations. Maybe, as the painter Larry Rivers says, this idea that art could tell us what was wrong with the world was "kind of dopey," but I believed it.

Their moral commitment is what kept me involved with the Beats all these years. Even when their own lives sometimes proved to be poor models of what they were trying to say, at least they were trying to say something. I photograph them and others in their company because they interest me. Once the Hungarian photographer André Kertész related a conversation with his comrades in the hospital after he was wounded in World War I. They asked him why he photographed the way their bodies appeared distorted in the water of the swimming pool. Kertész answered, "Why only girl friends? This also exists."

Beats & Company

Allen Ginsberg talking to Bob Dylan,
East Tenth Street, New York City, 1966

When I walked over to Allen Ginsberg's apartment on the Lower East Side in the spring of 1966 to talk to him about Jack Kerouac—and to take his picture as he talked to Bob Dylan—he was thirty-nine years old and solidly established as the dominant figure of the new literary underground. It was his poem *Howl*, published in 1956, that had broken through to a new consciousness of America with its famous opening line:

> *I saw the best minds of my generation destroyed by madness,*
> *starving, hysterical naked. . . .*

Ten years later *Howl* was in its sixteenth printing, and he had solidified his reputation in 1961 with *Kaddish*, a long, tender, deeply moving poem about the death of his mother, Naomi Ginsberg. Allen had grown up in Paterson, New Jersey, where his father Louis was a high school teacher. Louis Ginsberg was also a poet, but in a completely conventional style. One of the surprising things about Allen's life in the fifties and sixties was that despite serious differences with his father over their attitudes toward American society, they never lost contact with each other. Even when Allen was travelling incessantly, writing, publishing, reading, and lecturing, he managed to get to Paterson to visit his father. As John Clellon Holmes said about Allen, he is a respector of tradition, even if some people find his beliefs unconventional, a "tireless affirmer of the old continuities."

When I stood beside Ginsberg at Jack Kerouac's open coffin in Lowell, Massachusetts, at the funeral in October 1969, Allen looked at me and said, "I think Jack dreamed us all. . . ." I had the feeling instead that it was Allen who had brought the whole Beat Generation into being with the strength of his vision of himself and his friends as a new beginning—as a new generation. He wove the threads that kept them together, just as he held together the threads that tied his life and his art to the generations of poets before him—Blake, Whitman, Mayakovsky, William Carlos Williams—and to his father and to the memory of his mother Naomi.

> *No more to say, and nothing to weep for but the Beings in the Dream,*
> *trapped in its disappearance,*
> *sighing, screaming with it, buying and selling pieces of phantom,*
> *worshipping each other,*
> *worshipping the God included in it all—longing or inevitability?—*
> *while it lasts, a Vision—anything more?*

From *Kaddish*

Allen Ginsberg with his father,
Paterson, New Jersey, December 6, 1970

On December 6, 1970, I met Allen at his father's house in Paterson. He was scheduled to read his poems later that day at the Paterson Public Library, but before we went to the reading, I took photographs in the living room and on the front steps of the house, the father poet and the son poet coming together to pose stiffly side by side in the fading light of the winter afternoon.

Body, which I must soon resign,
Thank you for being briefly mine.

I used you, ere you're gathered under,
In an apprenticeship to wonder. . . .

I struggled in a rhyme to give
A home to what was fugitive.

So thanks again to have the loan
Of this ephemeral flesh and bone.

I tried the best I could to save
Some shining remnant from the grave.

Thanks for a Loan by Louis Ginsberg

With Allen through all the traveling and writing of these years was Peter Orlovsky, who had been my blind date in 1956 when he took me to the second reading of *Howl* in Berkeley. Peter and Allen had been living together since 1955, after Allen had walked into the apartment of artist Robert LaVigne in San Francisco and fallen in love with an "enormous, beautiful, lyrical, seven-by-seven-foot-square painting" in the room, a portrait LaVigne had painted of Peter. Peter's date with me was during a short period when he and Allen lived apart, seeing different people. As Allen said, Peter was primarily heterosexual, and "these things go in phases." They had been sharing their lives for more than a decade when I photographed Peter on East Tenth Street in New York City that afternoon in 1966. It was often Peter's calm practice of what friends called his "kitchen yoga" that gave a sense of order to their apartment in those years, with the hordes of strangers and friends, guests and lovers who visited and stayed with them.

Born in 1933, Peter was seven years younger than Allen. He had grown up in a poor family in Northport and Queens, New York, dropping out of high school when his mother told him she couldn't afford to feed him any longer so he had to go to work. Drafted into the Army during the Korean War, he was sent to a hospital in San Francisco and served as a medic. It was in San Francisco in 1954 that he met LaVigne and Ginsberg. Allen encouraged Peter to write poetry. At first he wrote only occasionally, but he began to chant and sing on stage with Allen during poetry readings after their return from India in 1963. His first book of poems was published eight years later. Poems come to Peter in "spontaneous flashes at odd moments & places," and he advises:

> *. . . just write out what*
> *you feel the most at one moment*
> *and you can't go wrong*
> *for you can just write out*
> *forever—the pen knows its job—*

Peter Orlovsky,
East Tenth Street, 1966

Jack Kerouac at Hyannis, Massachusetts, 1966

I'm sitting in my mother's arms in a brown aura of gloom sent up by her bathrobe—it has cords hanging, like the cords in movies, bellrope for Catherine Empress, but brown, hanging around the bathrobe belt—the bathrobe of the family, I saw it for 15 or 20 years—that people were sick in—old Christmas morning bathrobe with conventional diamonds or squares design, but the brown of the color of life, the color of the brain, the gray brown brain, and the first color I noticed after the rainy grays of my first views of the world in the spectrum from the crib so dumb. I'm in my mother's arms but somehow the chair is not on the floor, it's up in the air suspended in the voids of sawdust smelling mist blowing from Lajoie's wood yard, suspended over yard of grass at corner of West Sixth and Boisvert—that daguerreotype gray is all over, but my mother's robe sends auras of warm brown (the brown of my family)—so now when I bundle my chin in a warm scarf in a wet gale—I think on that comfort in the brown bathrobe—or as when a kitchen door is opened to winter allowing fresh ices of air to interfere with the warm billowy curtain of fragrant heat of cooking stove . . . say a vanilla pudding . . . I am the pudding, winter is the gray mist. . . .

From *Doctor Sax* by Jack Kerouac

Jack Kerouac with his mother Gabrielle

The excited, noisy, startlingly good-looking Jack Kerouac I had seen at the poetry reading in Berkeley in 1956 had changed so much ten years later—when I went to work on his bibliography with him in the small house in Hyannis, Massachusetts, where he was living with his mother in 1966—that when he opened the door in a rumpled T-shirt I thought confusedly that the man standing inside must be his father, even though I knew Leo Kerouac had been dead for twenty years. Kerouac had aged a lifetime since that first glimpse I'd had of him. I had the feeling that at the age of only forty-four in Hyannis he was already staring at the end of his life, but almost as though he didn't recognize himself in what was happening to him.

Howl was the first major breakthrough for the writers in the Beat group, but Kerouac's *On the Road,* published a year later in 1957, came the closest to describing their lifestyle, and with its success Kerouac was thrust into a role of describing and defending what they felt and lived. It wasn't a role he was comfortable with, but as John Clellon Holmes said later, with that novel Jack had made "a new crack in the consciousness, and everything else—pot, rock, doin' your thing, make a new Jerusalem—had come out of that crack."

Jack had written the first version of *On the Road* in three weeks on a 120-foot-long roll of teletype paper in a rush of benzedrine and coffee in an effort to explain to his second wife what his life had been like. He was so overwhelmed with it that he took it first to Holmes, then to publishers, in its original form as a roll of paper. This was in April 1951. When he finally was able to find a publisher for it six years later, his struggle to get the book published had so deeply scarred him that its success couldn't break the pattern of his life. He had always been emotionally dependent on his memories of his boyhood in Lowell, Massachusetts (the boyhood that was the subject of five of his books), and on his relationship with his mother. By 1966, an alcoholic, he was physically dependent on her as well.

As we worked together on his bibliography that weekend and talked about his books and why he'd written them, I realized that in some essential way he'd never left the Lowell of his imagination. Outside the house, when I photographed him kneeling beside his mother, the late afternoon was filled with bright summer sunlight. Inside the house I found only the darkness of his soul.

William Burroughs, London, December 1972

Once Gray Snyder said that he thought for a while that the Beat Generation was the lifestyle of four people—but in 1944, when Allen and Jack met William Burroughs, it was only three people, and they hadn't given any name to the way they were living. Burroughs was older—he had been born in 1914, twelve years before Kerouac, and he had graduated from Harvard in 1936—but he was as much adrift as they were. About the time they met—Allen was still a student and Jack was in the Merchant Marines—he became a morphine addict. At the same time that Burroughs was talking about books with Allen and Jack and encouraging them to be writers, he was introducing them to the scene he described in his first book *Junkie,* subtitled *Confessions of an Unredeemed Drug Addict* when it was published by Ace paperbacks in 1953 under the pseudonym William Lee.

From New York City he went to Louisiana, where Kerouac described him as "Old Bull Lee" in *On the Road,* then to Mexico, where in a drunken accident he shot his wife to death, and finally to Tangiers, where he wrote *Naked Lunch.* Kerouac typed up part of the manuscript from Burroughs' thousand pages of notes and gave the book its title. When it was published in 1959, it caused the same storm of controversy that *Howl* and *On the Road* had stirred up a few years earlier. As Kerouac said of it, the book "tried to make people shudder at their own lies . . . make them open up and be *straight* with one another."

I didn't have a chance to meet Burroughs until December 1972, when he was living in London. A couple of months after I'd photographed him, I went back to his apartment to show him the first copy of my newly published biography *Kerouac,* which the publisher had just airmailed to me from San Francisco. Burroughs stretched out a hand to take the book, turned without changing expression, and disappeared with it into a back room of the apartment. When he returned a short time later, he was empty-handed. He didn't mention the book and I never saw my copy again.

In 1948 when Kerouac was describing the way the hipsters walked in Times Square for John Clellon Holmes and came up with the term "beat generation," one of the people he was thinking about was a Times Square hustler named Herbert Huncke. Huncke was older than they were, he was much closer to street life, and he'd had much more experience with drugs. It was Huncke who led Burroughs into the underground world he described in *Junkie*. Burroughs gave him the name "Herman" in the book.

Huncke was already stealing to support a heroin habit, and the next year he was arrested for theft. He served time in Rikers Island, Sing Sing, Greenhaven, and Dannemora prisons before getting into a methadone program. Under Kerouac's influence he began to write journals and stories which Ginsberg thought were a "vehicle for a veritable new consciousness which spread to others sensitized by their dislocation from History." Huncke was more modest about his aims as a writer: "I try to tell the truth."

Since Huncke's work wasn't published until 1965, just before I met him, he was only a legendary name when I unexpectedly met him with Allen on the Lower East Side. I didn't have a camera with me that time, but an unknown fan had sent Allen an instamatic camera loaded with film that had just come in the mail while we sat in his kitchen and talked. The fan wanted a snapshot of Allen, so I volunteered to go out on the sidewalk with him and take it. Huncke came by just as we were leaving the apartment and he joined the picture-taking session. The loan of an unknown person's camera helped give the photographs a phantom quality that was part of the aura of mystery I already associated with Huncke. I sent the camera back with half a dozen snapshots of Ginsberg after I developed the film.

Herbert Huncke and Allen Ginsberg,
Lower East Side, New York City, 1966

The earliest Beat writing had New York City as its background, but in the 1950s the scene shifted to the West Coast. Kerouac and Ginsberg first went west in 1947, after they'd met Neal Cassady, who came to New York with his girlfriend Luanne. When Cassady, who was from Denver, went back again, Allen rode the Greyhound to Colorado to try and pick up his own love affair with Neal, and a few months later Kerouac hitchhiked out to join them. They soon went separate ways, but when Neal moved to San Francisco the next year, Kerouac began a series of trips back and forth across the country to see him, sometimes the two of them traveling together on the careening car trips that became the background for *On the Road*. In 1954 Ginsberg traveled west again by way of Mexico, and after a brief time living with Neal and his new wife and family, he found a job in San Francisco doing market research. Within a few months he met many of the writers who were part of the Bay Area's own literary "renaissance," and he also met Peter Orlovsky.

Although the Bay Area poets lived in as widely scattered places as Berkeley, Oakland, San Francisco, and Mill Valley, the center for what was happening was the North Beach neighborhood in San Francisco around Telegraph Hill. After Peter and Allen began living together early in 1955, they found a room on Montgomery Street where Allen wrote the first part of *Howl*. Close to Chinatown, North Beach had cheap apartments and residential hotels, with a string of bars and coffeehouses along Grant Avenue, and the City Lights Bookshop close to the corner of Columbus and Broadway.

In the fall of 1955 Ginsberg enrolled as a graduate student in the English Department at the University of California and found a one-room cottage on Milvia Street in Berkeley. He wrote Kerouac—who was living in Mexico City with an addict friend of Burroughs—to spend the winter with him. Jack arrived in time for the poetry reading that Allen organized at the Six Gallery in San Francisco on October 13. Allen had asked four local poets—Gary Snyder, Philip Whalen, Philip Lamantia, and Michael McClure—to read with him, and he persuaded Kenneth Rexroth to introduce them on stage. He read his poem *Howl* for the first time to a stunned and tumultuous response, and it was at that moment that the "Beat Generation" became part of the American Consciousness.

Among the people in the audience listening to the poets at the Six Gallery was Lawrence Ferlinghetti, one of the owners of City Lights Bookshop. Ginsberg had gone into the shop after he'd moved to North Beach and shown Larry a manuscript of some early poems. Ferlinghetti was just starting his own publishing company, City Lights Books, and the first title of his Pocket Poets series was scheduled to appear the next month, his own first book of poems, *Pictures of the Gone World.* After hearing Allen read *Howl,* Larry sent him a telegram echoing Emerson's letter to Whitman after he'd received his copy of *Leaves of Grass:* "I greet you at the beginning of a great career. When do I get the manuscript?"

Like most of the others in the early Beat movement, Ferlinghetti had roots in the East Coast—he was born in New York City in 1919—but he had taken his doctorate in literature at the Sorbonne. When he moved to San Francisco

Ferlinghetti in San Francisco, 1969

with his wife Kirby in 1949, he continued to be involved with the creative arts, writing and painting while he supported himself by teaching French literature at San Francisco State College and writing for *Art Digest* and the *San Francisco Chronicle*. He became involved with the San Francisco writers through Kenneth Rexroth's literary-anarchist sessions at Rexroth's Scott Street apartment. In June 1953 he opened City Lights Bookshop with a partner, Peter Martin, who left for New York and sold his interest back to Ferlinghetti just at the time the Pocket Poets Series was launched.

Without Ferlinghetti's support as a publisher the movement would have taken much more time to coalesce, and when *Howl*—number four in the Pocket Poets Series—was seized for obscenity in 1956, he fought the trial through the courts. In the book's defense he said, "It is not the poet but what he observes which is revealed as obscene. The great obscene wastes of *Howl* are the sad wastes of the mechanized world, lost among atom bombs and insane nationalism." And though it was never a role he felt particularly comfortable with, Ferlinghetti also became responsible for the writers when they came through town. If you wanted to get in touch with Allen or Jack, or with other poets like Gregory Corso who became part of the group, City Lights was the place to begin looking.

Ferlinghetti and Corso, San Francisco, 1969

Gregory Corso, another "jailkid" like Neal Cassady, had been sent to prison for robbery for three years when he was seventeen. When Ginsberg met him in 1951, he'd been out of jail only a few months. He'd begun reading in prison and was already beginning to write poetry himself. Gregory was from the Lower East Side in New York, where he grew up as much on the streets as he did in a series of unhappy foster homes. He was only casually attached to the group, and his poetry took on its own tone and voice. His first book, *The Vestal Lady on Brattle and Other Poems*, was financed in 1955 as a gesture of enthusiastic support by friends at Cambridge, where he was for a few months part of the Harvard scene.

In these early years he was on the road even more than the others. He lived a hand-to-mouth existence traveling in England, France, Germany, Italy, and Greece, sometimes running into Allen and Peter in places like Paris or Athens, then months later seeing them again in Chicago or San Francisco. In 1958 Ferlinghetti published his collection *Gasoline* as the eighth book in the Pocket Poets Series, and Gregory followed it with a brilliant pamphlet poem for City Lights, *Bomb*.

When I met Gregory in San Francisco in 1969 to take some photographs, he was on his way to City Lights. I spent most of the afternoon driving him from one errand to another, the same way many other people had done for him so many other times. It was a warm day and I didn't need to stay in the car all the time, so I began taking his picture wherever we happened to stop. Sometimes he seemed almost painfully conscious I was there; other times he forgot all about me and I caught sudden, unguarded looks that reflected the open spirit of his poetry.

Should I get married? Should I be good?
Astound the girl next door with my velvet suit and faustus hood?
Don't take her to movies but to cemeteries
tell her about werewolf bathtubs and forked clarinets
then desire her and kiss her and all the preliminaries
and she going just so far and I understanding why
not getting angry saying You must feel! It's beautiful to feel!
Instead take her in my arms lean against an old crooked tombstone
and woo her the entire night the constellations in the sky—

From *Marriage* by Gregory Corso

Gregory Corso, San Francisco, 1969

When Carolyn Robinson met Neal Cassady in 1947, she was a teaching assistant at the University of Denver, and she had no idea she would become part of a literary movement. After a chaotic courtship she married Neal in 1948, and Kerouac moved in with them for the first time in 1952, after they'd moved to San Francisco. She and Jack also became lovers, and he felt a closeness with her until the end of his life, even if finally the relationship only involved his drunken late-night phone calls and occasional letters. Despite the difficulties of her marriage with Neal—among other complications he served a term in San Quentin after he was set up in a narcotics arrest—she managed to raise their three children and work on her own projects in the arts and theater. After their deaths she wrote a memoir of her life with Jack and Neal, part of which was published in 1976 with the title *Heart Beat*. When I first met her in 1972, she was still living in the house she and Neal had bought together in Los Gatos, south of San Francisco.

Carolyn Cassady, 1982

Robert Duncan, San Francisco, 1969

Howl, with its trial on charges of obscenity, and *On the Road* cast a sudden glare of attention on the San Francisco literary scene, but there had been a community of writers, artists, filmmakers, printers, and musicians active there since the end of the Second World War. For most of them the publicity wasn't especially welcome, since they didn't think of themselves as part of Ginsberg and Kerouac's Beat Generation. At the same time, however, they shared the Beats' excitement at being part of the new cultural upheaval, and they had the same commitment to art and social change in what they regarded as the era of the nuclear apocalypse.

The dominant literary figure in all of this activity was Kenneth Rexroth, a poet, critic, translator, and political activist. When I was a student in Berkeley in the mid-1950s, it was Rexroth whom I heard and saw most often, reading his poetry over the radio or in jazz clubs, or striding along the San Francisco streets at parades and art festivals. He had come from Chicago in 1927, when he was twenty-two years old. A conscientious objector during World War II, he never gave up his radical political stance. It was to one of his Thursday night weekly seminars in his apartment that Ginsberg brought his letter of introduction from William Carlos Williams in 1955. From Rexroth's deep interest in Zen Buddhism, Oriental poetry, and radical politics came some of the ideas that influenced many Beat writers, including Ginsberg, Ferlinghetti, Snyder, Whalen, and McClure. In the first sweep of enthusiasm Rexroth was a strong supporter of Beat writing, but as the media began to focus more of its attention on Ginsberg, Kerouac, and Corso as "personalities," he became angry at what he called their lack of artistic discipline and kept his distance.

Robert Duncan and Brother Antoninus were part of a different group of poets living in Berkeley and San Francisco, but Duncan had been in New York for some years, where he was part of Anaïs Nin's circle, and he had been on the faculty at Black Mountain College. Antoninus was a gifted printer as well as a poet, and his presence in the group emphasized the West Coast tradition of finely printed small press books of poetry. At a reading in 1969 Antoninus stripped off his robes, left the Dominican order, and resumed his earlier identity as William Everson. Donald M. Allen, an editor, anthologist, and publisher, brought Beat and counterculture writing to a larger audience with his brilliantly edited anthology *The New American Poetry,* published in 1960. For the next few years I saw well-thumbed copies of the book in nearly every apartment I visited.

Kenneth Rexroth, San Francisco, 1969

57

Brother Antoninus, Kentfield Priory, 1969

Donald Allen, San Francisco, 1969

Philip Lamantia and Michael McClure were two of the other poets that Ginsberg asked to read at the Six Gallery. Lamantia was a young surrealist who had been part of the circle around André Breton in New York when he was still a teenager. His first book, *Erotic Poems,* was published in 1946, when he was nineteen. Michael McClure was an experimental poet who came to San Francisco from Kansas—by way of the University of Arizona—in 1952. His appearance at the Six Gallery was his first public reading. The young poet David Meltzer came to San Francisco from Los Angeles in 1957 in time to participate in the jazz and poetry readings that had become popular in North Beach. In part his writing has centered on his study of his Jewish identity, but he also shares many of the concerns and aesthetics of the other Bay Area poets.

Philip Lamantia, San Francisco, 1984

Michael McClure, San Francisco, 1969

David and Tina Meltzer, San Francisco, 1969

Gary Snyder, San Francisco, 1969

A few weeks after Ginsberg moved into his cottage in Berkeley in 1955, Rexroth introduced him to a graduate student in Oriental languages—"a bearded interesting Berkeley cat" as Allen described him in a letter—named Gary Snyder, who was living in another cottage not far from Ashby Avenue. The small, bare, unheated Berkeley cottages were a new scene for Allen and for Jack, who joined him in the fall. I was to move into my own tiny cottage on Forest Avenue a few blocks away the following year, and I still remember the raw, damp chill of gray winter days, the whir of the blade in my small electric heater fan, the taste of cheap California wine, my bicycle parked outside the door in the bamboo rushes, and the feeling that every weekend jazz and poetry were being newly invented everywhere around me.

Younger than Ginsberg, Snyder had graduated from Reed College and lived in the Bay Area awhile before they met. He read his poem *A Berry Feast* at the Six Gallery the night Ginsberg read *Howl*, and he was at the center of most of the parties and unending discussions that Kerouac described in *The Dharma Bums*. In the novel Jack romanticized Gary into the character named "Japhy Ryder," a characterization that Snyder has never been very happy with.

Several months after the Six Gallery reading, Snyder shipped out to Japan. He lived there for nearly a dozen years, studying Zen and meditation in Kyoto. He returned to the United States occasionally, once to be on the stage with Ginsberg at the great Human Be-In in San Francisco's Golden Gate Park in 1967. A year later he returned permanently to the United States with his Japanese wife Masa. They built a house and a meditation center in the mountains above California's Central Valley, where they live with their two children.

Deeply concerned with ecology and the future of the earth, Snyder writes poems and essays that have an increasing sense of engagement with these issues. When he and Michael McClure, with Michael's wife Joanna, came to Stockholm in 1972 to take part in an international ecological conference, they visited us in our house outside of the city so they could walk in a Swedish forest. I photographed him on a rock near our small lake while Michael went swimming. Gary said the water was too cold to go in: "Only a crazy paleface would have such a strange idea."

Coyote yaps, a knife!
Sunrise on yellow rocks.
People gone, death no disaster,
Clear sun in the scrubbed sky
                    empty and bright
Lizards scurry from darkness
We lizards sun on yellow rocks.

From *A Berry Feast* by Gary Snyder

Gary Snyder, Stockholm, Sweden, 1972

Michael McClure at a Stockholm lake with Gary Snyder, 1972

In 1955 Philip Whalen was working a summer job as a lookout in a fire station in the Cascade Mountains when his old Reed College roommate Gary Snyder wrote and asked him to come to San Francisco to read his poems with the other writers at the Six Gallery on October 13. It was Whalen whom Kerouac described as "Warren Coughlin" in *The Dharma Bums*. A San Francisco small press, Auerhahn, published Whalen's first book, *Self-Portrait from Another Direction*, in 1959. He stayed in Berkeley after Snyder left for Japan, but finally joined him there and lived in Kyoto for a few years teaching English. His immersion in Zen Buddhist studies began in San Francisco in 1970, and three years later he became the *Shuso*, head monk, at the Zen Mountain Center in Tassajara Springs. Along with his Zen studies he continues to develop his own idiosyncratic poetic style, not thinking of himself as a Beat, or even a modern, writer: "When I'm writing, I'm writing about what I know and what I want to write, I'm just doing what I want to do." He let me photograph him in the roof garden of the San Francisco Zen Center, surprised that I wanted to take his picture, but he obligingly took off his baseball cap when I asked him to.

Philip Whalen, San Francisco Zen Center, 1982

Joanne Kyger, Bolinas, 1982

Joanne Kyger came into the San Francisco literary scene from the University of California at Santa Barbara in 1957. She left before finishing her degree because she wanted to be a poet, so she found an apartment in North Beach and took a job as a secretary to support herself while she wrote. She became part of the circle of young poets around Robert Duncan and Jack Spicer. In 1958 she met Gary Snyder when he came to town to read from his new poems. Two years later she traveled to Japan to join him and they were married there. Her first book, *The Tapestry and the Web*, appeared in 1965, followed by several books of poetry and *The Japan and India Journals* (1960-1964), describing the years of their marriage. Since the 1970s she has lived on the mesa in Bolinas, a small coastal town north of San Francisco. Her small wooden house, filled with plants, is a center for the community of friends and writers in the neighborhood. At various times the Bolinas group has included Robert Creeley, Bobbie Louise Hawkins, Phil Whalen, Don Allen, Bill Berkson, Lewis MacAdams, Lewis Warsh, Ted Berrigan, Tom Clark, Richard Brautigan, and Aram Saroyan.

Diane di Prima in her apartment,
San Francisco, 1984

Whatever their sexual relationships between themselves, most of the Beat writers had the same feelings about women as any other men of the 1950s. If women came along, they were expected to sit quietly and listen, to laugh a lot, be sympathetic, and make sure there was something to eat. They were also expected to do the dishes and go to bed occasionally. They were definitely—as Joyce Glassman Johnson described in her book about her love affair with Kerouac—"minor characters."

But there was a young woman poet named Diane di Prima who didn't play the role as she was supposed to but insisted on having a voice of her own. Born in Brooklyn in 1934 with a conventional family background, she dropped out of Swarthmore College in her sophomore year and moved to Greenwich Village to share her life with a group of young poets, dancers, and artists. For her, reading *Howl* in 1957 was an overwhelming experience. "I knew that this Allen Ginsberg, whoever he was, had been breaking ground for all of us, though I had no idea yet what that meant, how far it would take us. . . . For I sensed that Allen was only the vanguard of a much larger thing. All the people who, like me, had hidden and skulked, writing down what they knew for a small handful of friends, waiting with only a slight bitterness for the thing to end, for man's era to draw to a close in a blaze of radiation—all of these would now step forward and say their piece. Not many would hear them, but they would, finally, hear each other. I was about to meet my brothers and sisters."

In di Prima's poetry she didn't try to imitate Ginsberg's style, but *Howl* gave her the courage that she could develop her own voice in any way she chose. In 1961 she published a book of prose poems about her life in the Village, *Dinners and Nightmares,* that so perfectly caught her wry tone of stubborn idealism and offhand humor that I wanted to buy a copy for every friend I had. Di Prima's place in the new group of poets involved more than her own writing. While she was living in the Village with LeRoi Jones, she began the *Floating Bear* newsletter, a monumental project she carried on for thirty-seven issues from 1961 to 1968. For each issue she gathered new poems and writing, mimeographed two or three hundred copies, and sent them free to anyone on her mailing list. *Floating Bear* became a way for the writers to keep track of the experimental work that they were doing, and almost everyone in the Beat group was included in one number or another. At the same time she was publishing books, pamphlets, and broadsides with her Poets' Press, she was running the Poets' Theater in the East Village, writing her own poetry, and raising her children.

In 1962 di Prima left New York City, living first in upstate New York, and then in Millbrook with Timothy Leary's group, before moving to California. She settled in an apartment in San Francisco around the corner from the Zen Center, and for the past several years she has taught at New College. She also gives many readings and continues to write and publish her own work.

It is still news to her that passion
could steer her wrong
though she went down, a thousand times
strung out
across railroad tracks, off bridges
under cars, or stiff
glass bottle still in hand, hair soft
on greasy pillows, still it is
news she cannot follow love (his
burning footsteps in blue crystal
snow) & still
come out all right

From *Loba* by Diane di Prima

Diane di Prima, San Francisco, 1984

It was in a conversation with John Clellon Holmes that Kerouac first described all of them as a "beat generation," and it was in an article for the New York *Times* four years later, "This Is the Beat Generation," that Holmes first tried to define the term for a larger audience. Already part of the group before it had a conscious identity, he first met Kerouac in 1948 at a party at Allen's apartment on York Avenue in Manhattan; he went along with the others to meet Neal Cassady when he arrived in New York with his girlfriend Luanne at Christmas that year; and he was the first to publish an autobiographical novel about their scene, his book *Go,* which appeared in 1952.

As close as Holmes was to the others, however, he always stayed just a step outside their circle. Born in 1926, he worked briefly in a Navy hospital during World War II (he is a pacifist) and studied philosophy at Columbia University after the war. He had already published in *Poetry* and *Partisan Review* before they all met. His work was closer to the literary mainstream than theirs, but he shared their passionate concern with experimental writing. He and Jack were particularly close friends, and in 1951 Holmes was the first person Kerouac asked to read the teletype-roll version of *On the Road.* At the same time, there was an element of competitiveness in their relationship. When Holmes received a twenty-thousand-dollar advance for *Go* a year later, Kerouac found it hard to accept John's success, since it threw his own difficulties in finding a publisher into even sharper relief.

Holmes never went hitchhiking with Jack or drove cross-country with Neal, and he didn't follow the rest of them to San Francisco. Instead he stayed in New York and then Connecticut with his second wife Shirley, publishing articles and two more novels. When he saw Allen or Jack, they were usually passing through, and as the years wore Kerouac down, it was finally only at Holmes' house in Old Saybrook where Jack could be sure he was welcome. No matter what shape he was in, John and Shirley were always ready to sit up and listen to him. Holmes' articles on Kerouac and the early Beat years collected in his books *Nothing More to Declare* and *Gone in October* are a sensitive, sympathetic record of their shared experience.

John Clellon Holmes, Old Saybrook, Connecticut, 1981

. . . with Shirley Holmes, Old Saybrook, 1985

GE M
FOUNTAIN ICE
NEWSPAPERS · MAGAZINES
IMPOR

EGG CREAM

ICE CREAM

MALTS

SODA

By the mid-1960s the original group of Beat writers had scattered. Allen and Peter traveled to Europe, Mexico, South America, and North Africa before settling for a time in India. Gary Snyder was mostly in Japan; Burroughs had left Mexico and was in Tangiers. With the income from his books, Kerouac bought his mother a series of houses on Long Island and in Florida before they moved in 1965 to a small, newly built Cape Cod house in back of a shopping mall in Hyannis, Massachusetts, far enough from New York City for him to have some privacy, yet close enough to Lowell for him to visit.

At the same time, however, a new scene was emerging in the Lower East Side in New York City. A new group of younger poets was living there, influenced partly by the Beats, but inspired also by the literary rebels of the previous generation—Ezra Pound, Gertrude Stein, and William Carlos Williams. Williams, who died in 1963 in Rutherford, New Jersey, had known Ginsberg as a young poet. He wrote the introduction to *Howl,* and one of his early experimental works, *Kora in Hell,* was reprinted as number seven in Ferlinghetti's Pocket Poets Series.

In the East Village, Ed Sanders, a young poet and political activist, was running the Peace Eye Bookstore on Tenth Street, where he edited *Fuck You/A Magazine of the Arts.* His first book, *Poem from Jail,* was published by City Lights in 1963. Along with Tuli Kupferberg and Ken Weaver, Sanders was also leading the Beats' only rock band, the Fugs. When I moved to the East

Village in 1965, they were playing down the street from me on St. Mark's Place, and I thought of them as my neighborhood band, marching with them down Fifth Avenue in an anti-Vietnam War protest parade the following year. Other neighbors in the East Village were Paul Blackburn and Ted Berrigan. Blackburn, who was translating Provencal poetry as well as writing his own poems, often turned up at McSorley's Old Ale House on Seventh Street, where I took his picture. His book *Brooklyn-Manhattan Transit* came out in 1970. Berrigan also lived close by on St. Mark's Place. Over the years he developed a loosely colloquial, open-ended poetry that drew on all of the older poets around for inspiration and sustenance, especially Ginsberg and the New York poet Frank O'Hara.

In the West Village, near Sixth Avenue, I met Louis Zukofsky, who had been one of the poets associated with Williams in the Objectivist group. In the 1960s Zukofsky was finally achieving recognition after forty years of going his own way as a writer.

Perhaps the best symbol for the new East Village community was the Gem Spa, at the corner of St. Mark's Place and Second Avenue, where we bought the Sunday New York *Times*, browsed for magazines, and ran into friends. Perhaps someone could make a point about the new cultural landmark being a newsstand and soda fountain instead of a bookstore or a cafe, but that didn't seem important at the time.

Ed Sanders and his daughter, New York City, 1966

Louis Zukofsky, New York City, 1966

Paul Blackburn, New York City, 1966

Anne Waldman came to live on St. Mark's Place on the Lower East Side in 1966, after her graduation from Bennington College, where she submitted her own poetry to partially fulfill the requirements of the Bachelor of Arts degree. Back in New York—she had grown up on MacDougal Street in the West Village—she started Angel Hair Press, publishing many of the new writers as well as her own work. Her first collection of poems, *On the Wing*, appeared in 1968. Much of her time went into working for the Poetry Project at St. Mark's Church in the Bowery, a community arts project which she directed from 1968 to 1977. She ran its writing workshops and readings, edited its newsletters, and organized its poetry fund-raising benefits. During these years the church at Tenth Street and Second Avenue became the center for most of the performance art in the East Village, featuring benefits to aid the anti-Vietnam War demonstrations and the regularly scheduled poetry readings which continue to the present day.

In 1975 Waldman left New York to work with Ginsberg setting up the Jack Kerouac School of Disembodied Poetics at the Naropa Institute in Boulder, Colorado. *Fast Speaking Woman*, her "most public book," was published that same year by City Lights. It became her most popular reading performance, composed in the spirit of the writers she calls her earliest "idols": Allen Ginsberg, William Burroughs, and Gregory Corso.

Anne Waldman, New York City, 1969

Everyone, it seems, is somewhere else.
          None are lost, tho. At least,
               we aren't!

                              (GEM'S SPA: corner of 2nd Avenue &
                                        Saint Marks Place)

●

I'm right here
Sunlight opening up the sidewalk,
Opening up today's first black&white,
& I'm about to be
born again thinking of you

From *Many Happy Returns* by Ted Berrigan

Ted Berrigan, Boulder, Colorado, 1982

Preceding page: Allen Ginsberg's farm,
Cherry Valley, New York, August, 1970

The Lower East Side, despite its sense of community, wasn't an easy place to live. It was crowded, dirty, drug and crime-ridden, discouragingly expensive, and often on the edge of chaos. To get out of it Ginsberg bought a small farm in Cherry Valley in the rolling hills of northern New York State, about 130 miles outside the city. He kept the Tenth Street apartment, but until he moved to Boulder, Colorado, in 1975 to teach at the Naropa Institute, the farm was home. With his usual generosity Ginsberg let as many people stay at the farm as the place would hold. The living arrangements were casual—the person most offended by the dirty dishes piled in the sink would wash them—but the farm functioned in its loose organization. Peter grew vegetables and tended his pet pig, while Allen had an easy relationship with most of his neighbors and ignored the FBI's wiretap on the telephone.

Julius Orlovsky in the kitchen at the Cherry Valley Farm

Ray Bremser, Cherry Valley, New York, 1970

Ray Bremser talking to his daughter. His wife Bonnie holds her close on her lap at the breakfast table.

Among the people living at the farm when I spent a weekend there in August 1970 were the poet Ray Bremser, his wife Bonnie, and their three-year-old daughter Georgia. Ray's first book, *Poems of Madness* (1965), was written while he served a six-year term at Bordentown Reformatory in New Jersey; his *Blowing Mouth/The Jazz Poems, 1958–1970* was influenced by Kerouac's poetry in *Mexico City Blues*. Bonnie Bremser's book *Troia: Mexican Memoirs* (1969) was her account of her life in Mexico with Ray before they came to stay on Ginsberg's farm.

When I stayed at Cherry Valley in 1970, Allen played the organ and sang his musical settings of William Blake's poetry to me in the parlor of the farmhouse after dinner. Nearly a dozen people were living in the house, but I remember how quiet it was that early evening in the country as Allen sang his songs, blending the tones of the organ and the sound of Blake's poetry into a single hosanna as he lost himself in the music.

For someone involved as I was in the new American writing in the 1950s and 1960s, there was another strong influence besides the Beats, another force that had its own aesthetics and direction. This was created by the group of writers, artists, dancers, and musicians who were together as teachers and students at the small experimental Black Mountain College near Asheville, North Carolina. Among the people whose work I liked who were associated with Black Mountain were Charles Olson, Robert Duncan, Robert Creeley, John Wieners, Merce Cunningham, John Cage, Harry Callahan, and Aaron Siskind. Olson was rector of the college when it closed in 1956. His own writing came from a highly personal stance involving an investigation of American history and a style of poetic inquiry he learned from Ezra Pound, but he was for Ginsberg, Duncan, and Creeley a dominant force in contemporary poetry, a major presence.

Olson, forty-six years old when Black Mountain closed, was from an earlier generation. Taking a long time to decide on his direction, he didn't publish his first collection of poems until 1953, only a few years before *Howl*. As much of an influence as his poetry on other writers, though, was his pamphlet called *Projective Verse*, published in 1959 and read by most of the poets of Ginsberg's generation. In this essay Olson introduced the idea of a poem as a field of energy based on the laws and possibilities of the "breath"—the free rhythm the Beats were all looking for in their own writing.

When I first met Olson in 1967 at the instigation of Berkeley publisher Robert Hawley, who asked me to write a critical study of the poet and his interest in Herman Melville, I found he was physically as large-dimensioned as his poems. Charles was six feet eight inches tall, a vast, jumbled man with a tumultuous energy that was as unpredictable as the Gloucester winds outside his window. I also found, over the next three years of our friendship, that he could hold his own under any circumstances. When Kerouac came to see him, Olson covered the kitchen floor with newspapers, including pages from a Boston paper that had a review of Jack's latest book. When Charles pointed it out, Jack called him some of the names he remembered from his Lowell boyhood. Olson answered him back with the same vocabulary. "I come from Worcester," he told me later, "and I know all the same words."

I have had to learn the simplest things
last. Which made for difficulties.
Even at sea I was slow, to get the hand out, or to cross
a wet deck.

       The sea was not, finally, my trade.
But even my trade, at it, I stood estranged
from that which was most familiar. Was delayed,
and was not content with the man's argument
that such postponement
is now the nature of
obedience,

         that we are all late
         in a slow time,
         that we grow up many
         And the single
         is not easily
         known. . . .

From *Maximus, to Himself* by Charles Olson

Olson's apartment in Gloucester

111

Larry Eigner is a poet born in 1927 who has been confined to a wheelchair, spastic since birth. Despite his physical handicap he has played an active role in the new literary underground through correspondence and his friendships with other poets. His writing is close in feeling to the spontaneity of the Beats and in technique to the open form poetry of the Black Mountain group. I photographed him at his parent's home in Swampscott, Massachusetts, where his typewriter was set up in a glass enclosed porch at the front of the house. Swampscott is close to Gloucester, and I often stopped to say hello to Larry on my trips to visit Charles Olson.

Allen Ginsberg and neighbor, Cherry Valley, 1970

113

Allen swinging Ray Bremser's daughter Georgia

The farmhouse

Peter Orlovsky at the Second LSD Conference,
Santa Cruz, 1981

Joyce Johnson is a novelist and author of the prize-winning memoir Minor Characters *about her love affair with Kerouac and her involvement in the Beat Scene in the 1950s. New York City, 1985*

The back steps to the apartment where Kerouac lived as a teenager in Lowell, Massachusetts. His family's apartment was on the top floor.

Kerouac's birthplace, Lupine Road, Lowell

Holmes, Ginsberg and Corso at Kerouac's funeral, Lowell, 1969

Ken Kesey at his farm in Oregon, 1984

The bus driven by Neal Cassady and the Merry Pranksters in the 1960s, now parked in Kesey's barn

Robert Creeley, Annisquam, Massachusetts, 1969

Robert Creeley was one of the writers who taught at Black Mountain College before it closed, and for years he maintained an extensive correspondence and friendship with Charles Olson. At the same time, he steadfastly stayed as close to Kerouac and Ginsberg and the other Beat writers. When Kenneth Rexroth had him briefly jailed in San Francisco after Creeley and Rexroth's wife ran off together, it was Kerouac who came to try to get him released.

Creeley, who had been writing and publishing books with his own small Divers Press before coming to Black Mountain, was set adrift by the collapse of his first marriage and the closing of Black Mountain. After a stop in New Mexico he came to San Francisco in 1956. Once there he immediately became part of what was happening, brought into the scene by the poet Robert Duncan, who had been at the college with him. As Creeley later described the time: "Great parties at Locke McCorkle's house out in Mill Valley—Allen and Peter charmingly dancing naked among a dense pack of clothed bodies, flowers at the prom! Jack and I sitting on the sidelines, shy, banging on upended pots and pans, 'keeping the beat.' Gary Snyder's wise old-young eyes, his centeredness and shyness also. Phil Whalen's, 'Well, Creeley, I *hope* you know what you're doing.' . . ."

One of the things that came out of Creeley's meeting with the new group of poets in San Francisco was a last issue of the *Black Mountain Review*, which he had been editing. In it he gathered new writing from both schools, and for the first time the Beats—Ginsberg, Kerouac, Burroughs, Snyder, McClure, and Whalen—were published together with the Black Mountain poets, among them Creeley himself. Bob has continued to move easily from one group of poets to the other, and his dual allegiance has never seemed to effect his own poetry, which has still the dry, allusive, compressed style of his first books.

When I first went to talk to Creeley and photograph him, he was staying in a small Cape Ann community not far from where Olson was living in Gloucester. I was surprised to learn, however, that their lives had involved them in so many other activities that despite their long relationship, they almost never met.

Bobbie Louise Hawkins was married to Robert Creeley for many years, and they still were together when I first talked to him in Annisquam in 1969. When I photographed her in Bolinas in 1982 she was continuing her own career as artist and poet.

The pallbearers entering the church with Kerouac's coffin.
Ginsberg is in the middle on the left.

Most of Kerouac's friends heard of his death on radio and television news broadcasts on the day after he collapsed with massive abdominal hemorrhaging in Florida on October 21, 1969. His body was brought back to Lowell, but only a few of the old group managed to get there in time for the funeral. Creeley drove down from Buffalo, where he was teaching, but he was so unnerved at seeing the cars parked outside the funeral home that he drove on past and went to a bar instead. He joined us for the church services the next morning. At the Archambault Funeral Home, Kerouac's body was on display in an open casket, a rosary chain crucifix wrapped around his folded hands. Allen, Peter and Gregory stood with their arms linked beside the casket, united with their old friend as a "team" for the last time. It didn't seem possible Jack was dead. I touched his forehead when Allen urged me to, so I would believe it. The next day the funeral services were conducted at St. Jean Baptiste Roman Catholic Church, where Kerouac had attended mass as a boy. The text for the funeral oration was based on a quotation from Ecclesiastes: "They shall rest from their words and take their works with them."

Jack Kerouac's funeral, Lowell, Massachusetts, October, 1969

At the end of the 1960s Kerouac was often disturbed that the Beats—a name that had metamorphosed into the much less positive journalists' term "beatniks"—were linked to the new generation of "hippies." But as much as he tried to deny it, the younger group had been spawned by ideas and attitudes in his novels, in Ginsberg's and Snyder's poetry, and in Burroughs' writing. One of the points of contact between the two generations was in the group around the novelist Ken Kesey, who startled the country in 1965 with the cross-country odyssey of his friends, the Merry Pranksters, in a rattletrap Day-Glo-painted bus with a destination sign reading "Further." The bus's driver was Neal Cassady.

Born in 1935, Kesey was thirteen years younger than Kerouac. He grew up in Oregon, and his first encounter with the Beats was reading *On the Road*. He read it three times, and it immediately effected his own writing. "When I first read Kerouac I headed off and *did* it. . . ." Struggling to make a living while he tried to write a novel, he worked for a while in a psychiatric hospital near Palo Alto, California, where he was a paid volunteer for an experimental government drug program, taking whatever kind of hallucinatory drug the government researchers gave him. When he enrolled in a writing course at Stanford University and worked with Malcolm Cowley, who had been Kerouac's editor for *On the Road* and was teaching the seminar, all of Kesey's experiences and influences coalesced into his novel *One Flew over the Cuckoo's Nest*. It was published in February 1962. The next fall he and his wife Faye came back to Palo Alto after a summer in Oregon and his life took a new turn. Neal Cassady, who lived close by, drove up to his house in a Willys Jeep with a transmission "blown from driving it too far too fierce too fast."

For the next few years Kesey lived through the beginnings of the 1960s counterculture, with the Merry Pranksters' "acid tests" and eventual drug troubles, which led to his flight to Mexico and arrest. He spent five months in detention in 1966 for possession of marijuana, and then he found himself even more notorious when journalist Tom Wolfe's description of the cross-country bus trip, *The Electric Kool-Aid Acid Test*, became a bestseller. At the end of their journey the Merry Pranksters went to find Kerouac in New York, but they had little to say to each other. It was the last time Jack and Neal met, but their old friendship had long since ended.

Preceding page: Ken and Faye Kesey,
Pleasant Valley, Oregon, 1984

In 1967 Kesey moved back to Oregon with Faye and their children. Since then he has written little that has been published. Most of the time he works on his farm taking care of the cattle, a solid, blocky figure on a tractor in the emptiness of the Oregon mountains. The Merry Pranksters' bus is in a barn on Kesey's farm, parked among his piled bales of hay. When I told him I'd ridden a Greyhound bus all night from San Francisco to visit him, Kesey shook his head. "What's the matter, too broke to ride the train?"

Kesey reading his morning mail

The summer of 1981 Ginsberg invited me to lecture with him on the Russian Futurist poets for a course he was giving on oral poetry titled "Wild Mouths" at the Jack Kerouac School of Disembodied Poetics he had established with Anne Waldman at the Naropa Institute in Boulder, Colorado. The summer program included many writing workshops and guest lectures, and while I was there I sat in on classes in American Indian poetry given by Joanne Kyger. After a class I photographed her with Ginsberg surrounded by some of their students.

The Beat poets and their friends continue to live in the Village and the Lower East Side, though some of them (Diane di Prima, Ed Sanders, Anne Waldman) have moved away from New York City and others (Paul Blackburn, Louis Zukofsky, Ted Berrigan) have died since I photographed them. Tuli Kupferberg, with Ed Sanders one of the founding members of the poetry-rock band the Fugs, stayed in New York with his wife and children and bought his apartment east of Sixth Avenue. The poet Alice Notley, Ted Berrigan's widow, lives with her two sons on St. Mark's Place and teaches a poetry workshop at St. Mark's Church nearby. John Giorno, a writer who is also involved in recording and filming poetry events on the Lower East Side, has an apartment on the Bowery named "the Bunker" by William Burroughs, who stays there when he visits New York. "The Bunker" is in the basement of an old building that used to house the downtown YMCA. Giorno has stripped the basement of its locker room facilities and showers, but he kept some of the toilets and urinals in the bathroom, where I photographed him opposite the apartment's only window.

Tuli Kupferberg, New York City, 1985

John Giorno, New York City, 1985

In "The Bunker"

Alice Notley, New York City, 1985

One Sunday in the summer of 1985 I dropped in to Allen Ginsberg's new apartment on East 12th Street and found Harry Smith there, the presiding spirit of music and poetry, recording the sounds coming from the church opposite the building. An artist and ethnomusicologist, Harry Smith was one of the first to reissue early blues records in the 1950s. Allen and I had the same favorite song on the monumental collection of American folk music Harry assembled for Folkways Records: Rabbit Brown's "James Alley Blues."

Gregory Corso, Melon Tytell, Robert Frank, "Jay," Lewis MacAdams, John Clellon Holmes at the Naropa Conference, Boulder, Colorado, 1982, celebrating the twenty-fifth anniversary of the publication of Kerouac's On the Road.

Eight years after founding the Jack Kerouac School of Disembodied Poetics at Naropa Institute, Ginsberg organized a summer conference in 1982 to commemorate the twenty-fifth anniversary of the publication of *On the Road*. Most of the writers associated with the Beats were invited to attend the conference to read their poetry and fiction, participate in lectures and panel discussions about Kerouac's life and work, and show films and play music. Scores of journalists and photographers converged on the event in Boulder, Colorado, along with the participants and spectators, because in the quarter century since the Beat writers had launched their literary movement they had earned considerable recognition for their achievement, including (collectively) the National Book Award, the Pulitzer Prize, Guggenheim Fellowships and NEA Grants, and membership in the American Institute of Arts and Letters. Suddenly it seemed that every journalist who could get to the conference wanted an interview. I took most of my photographs away from the crush of people who surrounded the writers, waiting until we returned to the old lodge where we were staying in the hills above Boulder. There on the porch we congregated for our own private twenty-fifth year reunion, talking among ourselves—usually in the company of Robert Frank, who had made the film "Pull My Daisy" with Kerouac, Ginsberg, Orlovsky and Corso in 1958, and who was photographing this conference too.

Prisoners of the Press Conference: Ginsberg, Waldman, Burroughs, Kesey—Naropa, 1982

Herbert Huncke, Jack Micheline, Michael McClure, and Carl Solomon on the porch at the Naropa Conference, 1982

Diane di Prima at the conference, sitting for a portrait by Robert LaVigne

Lawrence Ferlinghetti on the porch at the conference

Allen Ginsberg reading Howl *on the twenty-fifth anniversary of its publication, Columbia University, 1981.*

Short List of Books by Writers mentioned in
Beats & Company

1950   Jack Kerouac—*The Town and the City*

1952   John Clellon Holmes—*Go*

1953   William Burroughs—*Junkie*
        Larry Eigner—*From the Sustaining Air*
        Charles Olson—*The Maximus Poems 1-10*

1954   William Carlos Williams—*The Desert Music*

1955   Gregory Corso—*The Vestal Lady on Brattle*
        Lawrence Ferlinghetti—*Pictures of the Gone World*

1956   Allen Ginsberg—*Howl*
        Kenneth Rexroth—*In Defense of the Earth*

1957   Kerouac—*On the Road*

1958   Corso—*Gasoline; Bomb*
        Ferlinghetti—*Coney Island of the Mind*
        Holmes—*The Horn*
        Kerouac—*The Subterraneans; The Dharma Bums*
        Michael McClure—*Peyote Poem*
        John Wieners—*The Hotel Wentley Poems*

1959   Burroughs—*Naked Lunch*
        Robert Duncan—*Selected Poems*
        Kerouac—*Doctor Sax; Maggie Cassidy; Mexico City Blues;
                Pull My Daisy* (filmed by Robert Frank)
        McClure—*Hymns to St. Geryon*
        Olson—*Projective Verse*
        Gary Snyder—*Riprap*
        Philip Whalen—*Self-Portrait from Another Direction*

1960   Donald M. Allen (ed.)—*The New American Poetry*
        Paul Blackburn—*Brooklyn-Manhattan Transit*
        Duncan—*The Opening of the Field*
        Kerouac—*Tristessa*
        Frank O'Hara—*Second Avenue*
        Snyder—*Myths & Texts*
        Whalen—*Like I Say*

1961   Burroughs—*The Soft Machine*
        Diane di Prima—*Dinners and Nightmares*
        Ferlinghetti—*Starting from San Francisco*
        Ginsberg—*Kaddish*
        LeRoi Jones—*Preface to a Twenty Volume Suicide Note*
        Kerouac—*Book of Dreams*
        McClure—*Dark Brown*

1962   Burroughs—*The Ticket That Exploded*
        Corso—*Selected Poems*
        Robert Creeley—*For Love: Poems 1950-1960*
        Kerouac—*Big Sur*
        Ken Kesey—*One Flew Over the Cuckoo's Nest*
        David Meltzer—*We All Have Something to Say to Each Other*

1963   Burroughs and Ginsberg—*The Yage Letters*
        Ginsberg—*Reality Sandwiches*
        Kerouac—*Visions of Gerard*
        Ed Sanders—*Poem from Jail*
        Williams—*Paterson*

1964   Ted Berrigan—*The Sonnets*
        Burroughs—*Nova Express*

1965   Ferlinghetti—*Where Is Vietnam?*
        Herbert Huncke—*Huncke's Journal*
        Kerouac—*Desolation Angels*

Joanne Kyger—*The Tapestry and the Web*
McClure—*The Beard*

1966 Kerouac—*Satori in Paris*
Tuli Kupferberg—*1001 Ways to Beat the Draft*
Snyder—*A Range of Poems*
Carl Solomon—*Mishaps, Perhaps*

1967 Duncan—*The Truth and Life of Myth*
Holmes—*Nothing More to Declare*
Philip Lamantia—*Selected Poems*
Snyder—*The Back Country*

1968 Brother Antoninus (William Everson)—*The Residual Years*
Ginsberg—*Planet News*
Kerouac—*Vanity of Duluoz*

1969 Bonnie Bremser—*Troia: Mexican Memoirs*
di Prima—*Memoirs of a Beatnik*
Ferlinghetti—*Tyrannus Nix?*
Snyder—*Earth House Hold*

1970 Corso—*Elegiac Feelings American*
Snyder—*Regarding Wave*

1971 Neal Cassady—*The First Third*
di Prima—*Revolutionary Letters*
Meltzer (ed.)—*The San Francisco Poets*
Jack Micheline—*North of Manhattan*
O'Hara—*Collected Poems*
Rexroth—*American Poetry in the Twentieth Century*

1972 Ginsberg—*The Fall of America*
Kerouac—*Visions of Cody*

1974 McClure—*September Blackberries*
Snyder—*Turtle Island*

1975 di Prima—*Selected Poems 1956—1975*
Sanders—*Tales of Beatnik Glory*
Anne Waldman—*Fast Talking Woman*

1976 Carolyn Cassady—*Heart Beat: My Life with Jack and Neal*
1977 Neal Cassady and Allen Ginsberg—*As Ever: Collected Correspondence*

1978 Ray Bremser—*Blowing Mouth/The Jazz Poems, 1958-1970*
Burroughs—*Letters to Allen Ginsberg*
di Prima—*Loba*
Ginsberg—*Mind Breaths*
Peter Orlovsky—*Clean Asshole Poems and Smiling Vegetable Songs*
Waldman (ed.)—*Talking Poetics from Naropa Institute*

1980 Ginsberg and Orlovsky—*Straight Hearts' Delight*
Kesey—*The Day after Superman Died*
Huncke—*The Evening Sun Turned Crimson*
Snyder—*The Real Work: Interviews and Talks, 1964-1979*

1981 Burroughs—*Cities of the Red Night*
Corso—*Herald of the Autochthonic Spirit*
Alice Notley—*How Spring Comes*

1982 Ginsberg—*Plutonian Ode*
McClure—*Scratching the Beat Surface*
Olson—*The Maximus Poems (Complete)*
Snyder—*Axe Handles*

1984 Creeley—*Collected Poems*
Ginsberg—*Collected Poems*
Joyce Johnson—*Minor Characters.*

1985 Blackburn—*Collected Poems*
Holmes—*Gone in October*

Index of People in the Photographs